# The Future of Healthcare: Exploring Genomic Medicine for Students

Adonis Mark

Copyright © [2023]

# Title:The Future of Healthcare: Exploring Genomic Medicine for Students
## Author's: Adonis Mark

All rights reserved. No part of this publication may be reproduced, stored in a retrieval system, or transmitted in any form or by any means, electronic, mechanical, photocopying, recording, or otherwise, without the prior written permission of the publisher or author, except in the case of brief quotations embodied in critical reviews and certain other non-commercial uses permitted by copyright law.

This book was printed and published by [Publisher's: **Adonis Mark**] in [2023]

**ISBN:**

# TABLE OF CONTENT

## Chapter 1: Introduction to Genomic Medicine     06

The Basics of Genomic Medicine

History and Evolution of Genomic Medicine

Importance and Impact of Genomic Medicine

Ethical Considerations in Genomic Medicine

## Chapter 2: Understanding Genetics     14

Fundamentals of Genetics

DNA and Genetic Variation

Mendelian Inheritance Patterns

Genetic Disorders and Mutations

## Chapter 3: Genomic Technologies     23

Next-Generation Sequencing

Genome Editing and CRISPR-Cas9

Pharmacogenomics

Personalized Medicine and Precision Health

# Chapter 4: Applications of Genomic Medicine 33

Cancer Genomics

Genetic Testing and Counseling

Rare Genetic Diseases

Infectious Disease Genomics

Nutrigenomics and Lifestyle Factors

# Chapter 5: Genomic Medicine in Practice 44

Clinical Implementation of Genomic Medicine

Genomic Data Analysis and Interpretation

Integrating Genomic Medicine into Healthcare Systems

Challenges and Future Directions of Genomic Medicine

## Chapter 6: Ethics and Social Implications 52

Privacy and Data Protection

Genetic Discrimination

Genetic Engineering and Designer Babies

Access to Genomic Medicine

## Chapter 7: The Future of Genomic Medicine 60

Emerging Technologies and Innovations

Genomic Medicine for Global Health

Education and Training in Genomic Medicine

Public Engagement and Genomic Literacy

## Chapter 8: Conclusion and Reflections 68

Summary of Key Concepts

Personal Reflections on Genomic Medicine

# Chapter 1: Introduction to Genomic Medicine

## The Basics of Genomic Medicine

Welcome to the exciting world of genomic medicine! In this subchapter, we will introduce you to the fundamental concepts and principles that underpin this rapidly growing field. Whether you are a student of genetics or genomics or simply curious about the future of healthcare, this chapter will provide you with a solid foundation to explore the fascinating realm of genomic medicine.

Genomic medicine is a branch of medicine that utilizes knowledge of an individual's genetic makeup, or genome, to diagnose, treat, and prevent diseases. It is based on the understanding that our genes play a crucial role in determining our health and susceptibility to various conditions. By studying the entire genome or specific genes, scientists and healthcare professionals can uncover valuable insights that enable personalized, targeted healthcare.

To grasp the basics of genomic medicine, it is essential to understand the structure and organization of our genome. Our genome is composed of DNA (deoxyribonucleic acid), which is a long, twisted molecule found within the nucleus of our cells. DNA is made up of four chemical bases: adenine (A), cytosine (C), guanine (G), and thymine (T). The specific order of these bases forms the genetic code, which determines our unique traits and characteristics.

Genomic medicine encompasses several key areas, including genomics, pharmacogenomics, and genetic testing. Genomics refers to the study of an individual's entire genome, enabling researchers to identify variations and mutations that may be associated with diseases. Pharmacogenomics, on the other hand, focuses on how an individual's genetic makeup affects their response to medications. Genetic testing involves analyzing an individual's genes to detect the presence of certain genetic conditions or predispositions.

The applications of genomic medicine are vast and have the potential to revolutionize healthcare. From personalized medicine, where treatments are tailored to the individual's genetic profile, to the identification of genetic risks and the development of targeted therapies, genomic medicine holds great promise.

As students in the field of genetics and genomics, you are at the forefront of this exciting journey. By delving into the basics of genomic medicine, you will gain a solid understanding of the foundational concepts necessary to navigate this rapidly evolving field. So, come along as we explore the future of healthcare through the lens of genomic medicine!

## History and Evolution of Genomic Medicine

In the vast field of healthcare, few disciplines have garnered as much attention and promise as genomic medicine. This subchapter explores the history and evolution of this fascinating field, tracing its origins to present-day advancements that are revolutionizing the way we approach healthcare.

The journey of genomic medicine begins with the discovery of DNA's double helix structure by James Watson and Francis Crick in 1953. This breakthrough laid the foundation for understanding the genetic code, which ultimately led to the Human Genome Project in 1990. This ambitious endeavor aimed to map and sequence the entire human genome, a feat that was successfully accomplished in 2003.

The completion of the Human Genome Project unlocked a wealth of information, allowing scientists to identify specific genes associated with diseases. This knowledge laid the groundwork for the emergence of genomic medicine, which focuses on understanding how an individual's unique genetic makeup influences their health and susceptibility to diseases.

Advancements in sequencing technology have played a pivotal role in the evolution of genomic medicine. Initially, the process of sequencing a genome was a laborious and time-consuming task. However, with the advent of next-generation sequencing, it became possible to sequence an entire human genome in a matter of days, at a fraction of the cost.

The integration of genomic medicine into clinical practice has also seen significant progress. Once considered a niche field, genomics is now an integral part of patient care. Genetic testing has become more accessible, allowing individuals to gain insights into their genetic predispositions to various diseases. This knowledge empowers individuals to make informed decisions about their health and take proactive measures to prevent or manage certain conditions.

Furthermore, genomic medicine has revolutionized the field of precision medicine. By analyzing an individual's genetic profile, healthcare providers can tailor treatments to specific genetic variations, increasing their efficacy and minimizing adverse effects. This personalized approach to medicine has shown immense promise in the treatment of various cancers, rare genetic disorders, and cardiovascular diseases.

As genomic medicine continues to evolve, it holds immense potential for the future of healthcare. The integration of genomics with other cutting-edge technologies, such as artificial intelligence and big data analytics, promises to further enhance our understanding of diseases and improve patient outcomes.

In conclusion, the history and evolution of genomic medicine have been marked by remarkable discoveries and advancements. From the unraveling of the human genome to the integration of genomics into clinical practice, this field has transformed the way we approach healthcare. As students interested in genetics and genomics, understanding the history and evolution of genomic medicine will provide a solid foundation for exploring its future possibilities and the impact it can have on improving patient care.

## Importance and Impact of Genomic Medicine

In recent years, the field of genomic medicine has revolutionized the way we approach healthcare. By studying the unique genetic makeup of individuals, genomic medicine has the potential to provide personalized and targeted treatments for a wide range of diseases. This subchapter aims to explore the importance and impact of genomic medicine, specifically addressing the audience of students with a keen interest in genetics and genomics.

One of the most significant contributions of genomic medicine lies in its ability to uncover the underlying genetic causes of diseases. By analyzing an individual's genome, scientists can identify genetic variations that may predispose someone to certain conditions. This information allows healthcare professionals to assess an individual's risk, enabling early detection and prevention strategies. This proactive approach can significantly reduce the burden of diseases, improving both individual and public health outcomes.

Furthermore, genomic medicine has the potential to transform the field of drug development. Traditional drug discovery methods often rely on a trial-and-error approach. However, with the advent of genomic medicine, researchers can now tailor medications to an individual's genetic profile. This personalized medicine approach ensures that patients receive the most effective and safe treatments, minimizing adverse reactions and improving overall treatment outcomes.

Genomic medicine also plays a crucial role in the field of cancer research. By analyzing the genetic mutations present in cancer cells, scientists can develop targeted therapies that specifically attack these abnormalities. This precision medicine approach has shown promising results, leading to improved survival rates and better quality of life for cancer patients.

Moreover, genomic medicine is at the forefront of advancements in reproductive health. By analyzing the genetic makeup of embryos, scientists can identify potential genetic disorders before implantation, allowing parents to make informed decisions about their reproductive choices. This technology, known as preimplantation genetic testing, has revolutionized assisted reproductive techniques and has the potential to prevent the transmission of genetic diseases to future generations.

In conclusion, genomic medicine has immense importance and impact in the realm of healthcare. It has the potential to revolutionize disease prevention, drug development, cancer research, and reproductive health. As students with a keen interest in genetics and genomics, it is crucial to understand the advancements in genomic medicine and its potential to shape the future of healthcare. By embracing genomic medicine, we can unlock a new era of personalized and targeted treatments, ultimately improving patient outcomes and enhancing the overall well-being of society.

# Ethical Considerations in Genomic Medicine

In recent years, the field of genomic medicine has witnessed remarkable advancements, offering immense potential for improving healthcare outcomes. As students in the fields of genetics and genomics, it is essential to explore the ethical considerations surrounding the use of genomic medicine. These considerations encompass a wide array of topics, including privacy, informed consent, genetic discrimination, and the equitable distribution of genomic technologies.

One of the foremost ethical concerns in genomic medicine is the issue of privacy. Genomic data contains highly personal and sensitive information, raising questions about who should have access to this data and how it should be protected. As students, it is crucial to understand the importance of maintaining patient confidentiality and implementing robust security measures to safeguard genomic information from unauthorized access or misuse.

Informed consent is another critical ethical consideration in genomic medicine. Before undergoing genetic testing or receiving genomic-based treatments, individuals must fully understand the potential risks, benefits, and limitations involved. Students should be aware of the challenges in obtaining informed consent, particularly in cases where children or individuals with impaired decision-making capacity are involved. Additionally, there is a need for clear guidelines on how to handle incidental findings, unexpected genetic information that may be discovered during genomic testing.

Genetic discrimination poses a significant ethical concern in the realm of genomic medicine. This form of discrimination occurs when individuals are treated unfairly based on their genetic information, such as denial of employment or insurance coverage. As future professionals in genetics and genomics, students must advocate for legislation that protects individuals from genetic discrimination and work to educate the public about the importance of genetic nondiscrimination.

Lastly, the equitable distribution of genomic technologies is a pressing ethical consideration. Genomic medicine has the potential to revolutionize healthcare, but its availability should not be limited to a privileged few. Students should strive to address disparities in access to genomic technologies, ensuring that advancements in this field are accessible and affordable to all populations, regardless of socioeconomic status or geographic location.

In conclusion, as students in the field of genetics and genomics, it is vital to consider the ethical implications of genomic medicine. By addressing concerns related to privacy, informed consent, genetic discrimination, and equitable distribution, we can contribute to the responsible and ethical advancement of genomic medicine. As future professionals, we have the power to shape the future of healthcare, ensuring it is based on the principles of justice, respect for autonomy, and equal access for all.

# Chapter 2: Understanding Genetics

**Fundamentals of Genetics**

Title: Fundamentals of Genetics

Introduction:
Welcome to the exciting world of genetics! In this subchapter, we will delve into the fundamentals of genetics, an essential branch of biology that explores the inheritance and variation of traits. Understanding genetics is crucial in the field of genomics, which is revolutionizing healthcare. Whether you are a student of genetics or genomics, this subchapter will lay a strong foundation for your learning journey.

1. What is Genetics?
Genetics is the study of genes, heredity, and genetic variation in living organisms. Genes are segments of DNA that carry instructions for building and maintaining an organism. Genetic information is passed down from one generation to the next, influencing our physical traits, diseases, and even our response to medications.

2. Mendelian Inheritance:
Gregor Mendel, the father of genetics, discovered the basic principles of inheritance. He observed that certain traits are inherited in predictable patterns through generations. We will explore Mendel's laws of inheritance, including dominant and recessive traits, Punnett squares, and the concept of alleles.

3. DNA and Genes:
Understanding the structure and function of DNA is crucial in genetics. We will explore the double-helix structure of DNA, the role

of DNA in gene expression, and how mutations can occur, leading to genetic disorders. Additionally, we will discuss the Human Genome Project, which mapped the entire human genome and opened doors to personalized medicine.

4. Chromosomes and Genetic Disorders: Chromosomes are thread-like structures that carry genes. We will learn about the different types of chromosomes and their role in determining an individual's sex. Additionally, we will discuss common genetic disorders, such as Down syndrome, cystic fibrosis, and sickle cell anemia, and how they are inherited.

5. Genetic Testing and Counseling: Advances in genomics have led to the development of genetic testing, which can detect genetic disorders and predict the risk of certain diseases. We will explore the types of genetic tests, ethical considerations, and the role of genetic counseling in helping individuals make informed decisions about their genetic health.

Conclusion:
Understanding the fundamentals of genetics is essential for anyone interested in the field of genomics and its applications in healthcare. By grasping the principles of inheritance, DNA structure, and genetic disorders, students can embark on a journey of discovery and contribute to the future of healthcare. Genetics and genomics hold immense potential in unlocking personalized treatments, disease prevention, and improving overall patient care.

## DNA and Genetic Variation

One of the most fascinating aspects of genetics and genomics is the concept of DNA and genetic variation. DNA, or deoxyribonucleic acid, is the molecule that contains the instructions for the development and functioning of all living organisms. It is often referred to as the "blueprint of life."

In this subchapter, we will delve into the world of DNA and explore the significance of genetic variation. Genetic variation refers to the differences in DNA sequences between individuals, which can be responsible for the diversity observed in traits, susceptibility to diseases, and response to medications.

The discovery of the structure of DNA by James Watson and Francis Crick in 1953 was a groundbreaking moment in scientific history. This double-helix structure, composed of nucleotides, serves as the foundation for all genetic information. Understanding DNA has allowed scientists to unravel the mysteries of heredity and genetics.

Genetic variation occurs due to several factors. Mutations, which are changes in the DNA sequence, can arise spontaneously or be induced by environmental factors. Genetic recombination during sexual reproduction also contributes to variation as genes from both parents are mixed and reshuffled to create new combinations.

The impact of genetic variation is far-reaching. It influences our physical traits, such as eye color, height, and hair texture. Additionally, genetic variation plays a critical role in determining our susceptibility to diseases. Certain genetic variations can increase the risk of developing disorders like cancer, heart disease, or diabetes. On the other hand, some genetic variations can provide protection against certain diseases.

Understanding genetic variation is essential in the field of medicine. It helps researchers identify genetic markers associated with various diseases, enabling the development of targeted therapies and personalized medicine. Genetic testing has become increasingly common, allowing individuals to learn about their genetic makeup and potential health risks.

Moreover, genetic variation has implications for evolutionary biology. It is the driving force behind natural selection, allowing species to adapt to changing environments over time.

As students interested in genetics and genomics, understanding DNA and genetic variation is fundamental to your journey. It opens the door to a world of possibilities, from unraveling the mysteries of our own biology to contributing to groundbreaking discoveries in medicine.

In the following chapters, we will explore the techniques used to study genetic variation, the impact of genetic variation on human health, and the ethical considerations surrounding genetic research. Get ready to embark on an exciting exploration of the future of healthcare through the lens of genomic medicine.

## Mendelian Inheritance Patterns

In the fascinating realm of genetics and genomics, one of the fundamental concepts that students must grasp is Mendelian inheritance patterns. Named after Gregor Mendel, an Augustinian friar and scientist, this theory lays the groundwork for understanding how traits are passed down from parents to offspring.

Mendelian inheritance patterns revolve around the idea that genes are inherited in a predictable manner, following specific rules. These rules govern the transmission of traits and help us unravel the mysteries of inheritance. By understanding these patterns, we can gain insights into the likelihood of certain traits appearing in future generations.

One of the most basic principles of Mendelian inheritance is the concept of dominant and recessive alleles. Alleles are alternative forms of a gene that determine specific traits. Dominant alleles are expressed when present, overshadowing the expression of recessive alleles. For example, if an individual has a dominant allele for brown eyes and a recessive allele for blue eyes, their eye color will be brown.

Another important concept in Mendelian inheritance is that of genotype and phenotype. Genotype refers to the genetic makeup of an individual, while phenotype refers to the observable characteristics. While the genotype determines the potential for certain traits, the phenotype is the result of how those genes are expressed.

Mendelian inheritance patterns can be further classified into different types, such as autosomal dominant, autosomal recessive, X-linked dominant, and X-linked recessive, among others. These patterns determine the likelihood of inheriting specific traits or disorders and can be depicted using Punnett squares, a visual tool that predicts the probability of offspring inheriting certain traits.

Understanding Mendelian inheritance patterns is crucial in the field of genomics and has far-reaching implications for healthcare. By studying these patterns, scientists can identify genetic disorders, develop targeted treatments, and provide personalized medicine. Furthermore, it helps individuals make informed decisions about their health and allows for genetic counseling to assess the risk of passing on genetic conditions to future generations.

In conclusion, Mendelian inheritance patterns form the foundation of our understanding of how traits are passed down through generations. By unraveling these patterns, students in the field of genetics and genomics can gain insights into the complexities of inheritance and pave the way for advancements in healthcare.

# Genetic Disorders and Mutations

Introduction:
In the fascinating world of genetics and genomics, one of the most intriguing aspects is the study of genetic disorders and mutations. Genetic disorders are conditions caused by changes or abnormalities in an individual's DNA. These disorders can have a profound impact on an individual's health and well-being. In this subchapter, we will dive into the intriguing world of genetic disorders and explore the role of mutations in shaping human health.

Understanding Genetic Disorders:
Genetic disorders can be inherited from parents or arise spontaneously due to mutations. There are thousands of known genetic disorders, ranging from relatively common ones like Down syndrome to rare conditions such as Hutchinson-Gilford progeria syndrome. We will explore some of the most well-known genetic disorders and discuss their causes, symptoms, and impact on individuals' lives.

The Role of Mutations:
Mutations play a crucial role in genetic disorders. They are spontaneous changes in DNA that can occur during DNA replication or as a result of environmental factors. Mutations can either be harmful, leading to genetic disorders, or beneficial, driving evolution. We will explore different types of mutations, such as point mutations, insertions, and deletions, and understand how they can disrupt normal gene function.

Inheritance Patterns:
Understanding how genetic disorders are inherited is essential. We

will explain the different inheritance patterns, including autosomal dominant, autosomal recessive, and X-linked inheritance. This knowledge will help students grasp the likelihood of inheriting a genetic disorder and the importance of genetic counseling in families with a history of genetic conditions.

Genetic Testing and Diagnosis: Advancements in genomics have revolutionized the diagnosis of genetic disorders. We will discuss the various techniques and tests used to diagnose genetic disorders, including prenatal testing, carrier screening, and whole-genome sequencing. This section will highlight the importance of early diagnosis for effective management and treatment of genetic disorders.

Treatment and Management: While some genetic disorders have no cure, advancements in medical research have led to innovative treatment approaches. We will explore different strategies for managing genetic disorders, including gene therapy, enzyme replacement therapy, and lifestyle modifications. Students will gain insight into the ongoing efforts to develop targeted treatments for genetic disorders.

Future Perspectives: The future of healthcare heavily relies on genomics and precision medicine. We will highlight the promising advancements in genetic research, including CRISPR gene editing and personalized medicine. Students will be inspired by the potential of genomics to transform healthcare and improve the lives of individuals affected by genetic disorders.

Conclusion:

Genetic disorders and mutations are captivating topics within the realm of genetics and genomics. Understanding the causes, inheritance patterns, and treatment options for genetic disorders is instrumental in shaping the future of healthcare. With ongoing advancements in genomic medicine, students have a unique opportunity to contribute to the field and make a positive impact on the lives of individuals affected by genetic disorders.

# Chapter 3: Genomic Technologies

## Next-Generation Sequencing

Next-Generation Sequencing: Unlocking the Secrets of Genomic Medicine

In the rapidly advancing field of healthcare, one technology has emerged as a game-changer, revolutionizing the way we understand genetics and genomics. This groundbreaking innovation is called Next-Generation Sequencing (NGS). In this subchapter, we will explore the incredible potential of NGS and its significance in the future of healthcare.

NGS is a cutting-edge method that allows scientists to decode the entire human genome, revealing a wealth of information about an individual's genetic makeup. This technology has the power to unravel the mysteries of inherited diseases, predict the risk of developing certain conditions, and guide personalized treatment plans.

So, how does NGS work? Traditional DNA sequencing methods were time-consuming and expensive, limited to analyzing small sections of the genome at a time. NGS, on the other hand, enables high-speed, large-scale sequencing of DNA, enabling researchers to sequence entire genomes in a matter of days. This breakthrough has made genetic testing more accessible and affordable, paving the way for personalized medicine.

One of the most significant applications of NGS lies in the field of precision medicine. By analyzing an individual's genetic code, doctors can tailor treatment plans to match a patient's unique genetic profile, maximizing effectiveness while minimizing side effects. This approach has revolutionized oncology, allowing for targeted therapies that attack cancer cells specifically, leading to improved outcomes and survival rates.

NGS also holds immense potential in the diagnosis of genetic disorders. By comparing an individual's DNA with a comprehensive database of known genetic variations, doctors can identify the specific genetic mutations responsible for a particular condition. This knowledge not only aids in accurate diagnosis but also facilitates genetic counseling and family planning for individuals and families at risk.

Moreover, NGS has opened new doors in the field of research, enabling scientists to study the genetic basis of various diseases more comprehensively. This, in turn, facilitates the development of novel therapies and interventions, bringing us closer to finding cures for previously untreatable conditions.

As students interested in genetics and genomics, understanding the power and potential of NGS is crucial. This technology is at the forefront of medical breakthroughs, offering incredible opportunities for advancements in healthcare. As the field of genomics continues to evolve, NGS will undoubtedly play a pivotal role in shaping the future of medicine, providing hope and improved outcomes for patients worldwide.

In conclusion, Next-Generation Sequencing is a revolutionary tool that has transformed the field of genomics. Its ability to rapidly decode the entire human genome has opened doors to personalized medicine, accurate diagnosis of genetic disorders, and groundbreaking research. As students, embracing this technology and its implications will undoubtedly shape our careers and the future of healthcare.

## Genome Editing and CRISPR-Cas9

Genetic engineering has revolutionized the field of healthcare, offering unprecedented opportunities for treating and preventing diseases. One of the most promising advancements in this realm is the development of genome editing techniques, with CRISPR-Cas9 leading the way. In this subchapter, we will delve into the fascinating world of genome editing and explore the remarkable potential of CRISPR-Cas9.

Genome editing refers to the precise modification of an organism's DNA, allowing scientists to add, remove, or alter specific genetic material. This breakthrough technology has opened up endless possibilities for the treatment of genetic disorders, as well as the development of more resilient crops and livestock.

At the forefront of genome editing techniques is CRISPR-Cas9, a revolutionary tool that has taken the scientific community by storm. CRISPR, short for Clustered Regularly Interspaced Short Palindromic Repeats, is a natural defense mechanism found in bacteria that helps them fight off viral infections. Scientists have harnessed this system and combined it with Cas9, an enzyme that acts as a pair of molecular scissors, to create a powerful tool for precise genetic editing.

CRISPR-Cas9 works by using a guide RNA to direct the Cas9 enzyme to a specific target sequence in the DNA. Once there, Cas9 cuts the DNA, allowing for the introduction of new genetic material or repair of existing genes. This technique has the potential to cure genetic diseases, as it enables scientists to correct faulty genes responsible for various disorders.

The impact of CRISPR-Cas9 on medicine and healthcare is immense. It has the potential to revolutionize the treatment of diseases like cancer, HIV, and sickle cell anemia. By precisely editing the genetic material in affected cells, scientists can potentially eliminate the root cause of these diseases, offering hope for millions of patients worldwide.

However, with great power comes great responsibility. The ethical implications of genome editing are complex and require careful consideration. The potential for misuse or unintended consequences raises questions about the ethical boundaries of altering the human genome.

As students of genetics and genomics, it is critical to understand the immense potential of genome editing and CRISPR-Cas9, while also being aware of the ethical challenges they pose. The future of healthcare lies in the hands of those who are knowledgeable, responsible, and compassionate. By exploring genomic medicine, we can contribute to the advancement of healthcare and shape a better future for all.

## Pharmacogenomics

Pharmacogenomics is a rapidly evolving field that combines the study of genetics and genomics with the practice of medicine. It explores how an individual's genetic makeup can influence their response to drugs, helping healthcare professionals tailor treatment plans to each patient's unique genetic profile. In this subchapter, we will delve into the fascinating world of pharmacogenomics and its potential to revolutionize healthcare.

Understanding how different individuals respond to drugs is crucial for optimizing treatment outcomes. Traditionally, a "one size fits all" approach has been taken, where medications are prescribed based on average responses observed in a large population. However, this approach fails to account for the considerable genetic variation among individuals, leading to adverse drug reactions or ineffective treatments. Pharmacogenomics aims to address this issue by identifying genetic markers that can predict an individual's response to a specific drug.

By analyzing an individual's genetic variations, scientists can identify specific genes that play a role in drug metabolism, efficacy, and toxicity. These genetic markers can help healthcare professionals determine the most suitable medication, dosage, and treatment duration for a patient, maximizing the chances of a positive response while minimizing adverse side effects.

One remarkable example of pharmacogenomics in action is the identification of the TPMT gene variant, which affects the metabolism of the drug azathioprine. Individuals with certain genetic variants of TPMT have an increased risk of experiencing severe bone marrow toxicity when taking this medication. By analyzing a patient's TPMT genotype before prescribing azathioprine, healthcare professionals can now customize the dose to minimize the risk of adverse reactions.

The future of pharmacogenomics holds tremendous potential. As genomic medicine continues to advance, we can expect more comprehensive genetic tests that cover a wider range of drugs. This expansion will allow healthcare professionals to provide personalized treatment plans for various conditions, such as cancer, cardiovascular diseases, and mental health disorders.

Pharmacogenomics also offers the possibility of developing new drugs that are specifically designed to target individual genetic variations, enhancing their efficacy and reducing side effects. This approach, known as precision medicine, aims to revolutionize healthcare by tailoring treatments based on an individual's genetic blueprint.

In conclusion, pharmacogenomics is a groundbreaking field that combines genetics, genomics, and medicine to optimize treatment outcomes. By understanding how an individual's genetic makeup influences their response to drugs, healthcare professionals can provide personalized treatment plans that maximize efficacy while minimizing adverse reactions. As students exploring the world of genetics and genomics, the knowledge of pharmacogenomics will undoubtedly play a crucial role in shaping the future of healthcare.

# Personalized Medicine and Precision Health

In recent years, the field of medicine has witnessed a remarkable transformation with the advent of personalized medicine and precision health. These cutting-edge approaches are revolutionizing the way we understand and treat diseases, offering new hope for patients and opening up exciting opportunities for healthcare professionals.

Personalized medicine is a groundbreaking approach that takes into account an individual's unique genetic makeup, lifestyle, and environment to tailor medical treatments and interventions. By analyzing an individual's DNA, scientists and healthcare providers can gain valuable insights into their susceptibility to certain diseases, their response to specific medications, and even their predisposition to adverse drug reactions. This information allows for the development of personalized treatment plans that are more effective, safer, and better suited to each patient's needs.

Precision health, on the other hand, focuses on identifying and addressing the root causes of diseases, rather than just managing their symptoms. By using advanced technologies, such as genomics and big data analytics, precision health aims to predict, prevent, and treat diseases at the individual level. It takes into account various factors such as genetics, lifestyle choices, environmental exposures, and social determinants of health, to develop comprehensive strategies that promote optimal health and well-being.

For students interested in genetics and genomics, personalized medicine and precision health offer a wealth of opportunities.

Understanding the role of genetics in disease susceptibility and treatment response is crucial for developing targeted therapies that can truly make a difference in patients' lives. By studying the intricate workings of the human genome, students can contribute to the development of novel diagnostic tools, therapeutic interventions, and preventive strategies that can transform healthcare as we know it.

Moreover, the integration of genetics and genomics into clinical practice requires a multidisciplinary approach. Students with backgrounds in genetics, medicine, nursing, bioinformatics, and other related fields can work collaboratively to unravel the complexities of human biology and translate scientific discoveries into clinical applications. This interdisciplinary collaboration is essential for advancing personalized medicine and precision health and maximizing their potential to improve patient outcomes.

As students, it is crucial to stay updated with the latest developments in this rapidly evolving field. The Future of Healthcare: Exploring Genomic Medicine for Students provides a comprehensive overview of personalized medicine and precision health, explaining the underlying principles, technologies, and ethical considerations. It also highlights the diverse career opportunities available in genetics and genomics, inspiring students to pursue further studies and research in this exciting field.

The era of personalized medicine and precision health has dawned, and students have a pivotal role to play in shaping its future. By harnessing the power of genetics and genomics, we have the potential to transform healthcare into a more precise, proactive, and patient-centered discipline. So, dive into the world of personalized medicine and precision health, and embark on a journey that will redefine the future of healthcare for generations to come.

# Chapter 4: Applications of Genomic Medicine

## Cancer Genomics

Cancer is a complex disease that affects millions of people worldwide. It is characterized by uncontrolled cell growth and the ability of cancer cells to invade other tissues. While there have been significant advancements in the diagnosis and treatment of cancer, researchers are constantly searching for new ways to improve outcomes for patients. One promising field that holds great potential in the fight against cancer is cancer genomics.

Cancer genomics is the study of the genetic changes that occur in cancer cells. By analyzing the DNA and RNA of tumor samples, scientists can identify specific mutations and alterations that drive the development and progression of cancer. This knowledge can help in understanding the underlying causes of cancer, identifying potential therapeutic targets, and developing personalized treatment strategies.

One of the key advancements in cancer genomics is the development of next-generation sequencing technologies. These technologies allow researchers to rapidly sequence the entire genome of cancer cells, providing a comprehensive view of the genetic landscape of a tumor. This has led to the discovery of numerous cancer-associated genes and an improved understanding of the molecular basis of different types of cancer.

With the advent of cancer genomics, researchers have also been able to classify tumors based on their genetic profiles rather than just their tissue of origin. This has led to the identification of subtypes within certain cancers, each with its own unique genetic characteristics. By understanding these subtypes, doctors can tailor treatment plans to be more effective and precise, leading to better patient outcomes.

Additionally, cancer genomics has paved the way for the development of targeted therapies. These therapies are designed to specifically target the genetic alterations present in cancer cells, while sparing healthy cells. This approach has shown great promise in the treatment of several cancers, with improved response rates and fewer side effects compared to traditional chemotherapy.

As students interested in genetics and genomics, understanding the field of cancer genomics is crucial. It not only provides a fascinating insight into the molecular mechanisms of cancer but also offers hope for the future of cancer treatment. By studying cancer genomics, you can contribute to the ongoing efforts to unravel the complexities of cancer and ultimately make a difference in the lives of patients.

In conclusion, cancer genomics is a rapidly evolving field that holds immense potential in the fight against cancer. Through the use of advanced sequencing technologies and the analysis of genetic alterations, researchers are gaining a deeper understanding of the molecular basis of cancer. This knowledge is driving the development of targeted therapies and personalized treatment strategies, which have the potential to revolutionize cancer care. As students interested in genetics and genomics, exploring the field of cancer genomics can provide valuable insights and open doors to exciting career opportunities in the future of healthcare.

## Genetic Testing and Counseling

Welcome to the subchapter on Genetic Testing and Counseling! In this section, we will explore the fascinating field of genetics and genomics and how it impacts healthcare. As students interested in genetics and genomics, you are taking a step towards understanding the future of healthcare and the role of genomic medicine.

Genetic testing is a powerful tool that allows us to analyze an individual's DNA to identify changes or mutations in their genes. These tests can provide valuable information about an individual's risk of developing certain genetic disorders or their likelihood of passing those disorders to their children. The testing process involves collecting a sample, often through a simple blood or saliva test, and analyzing the DNA in a laboratory. The results can help healthcare professionals make informed decisions about prevention, early detection, and treatment options.

However, genetic testing is not just about predicting diseases; it also plays a crucial role in personalized medicine. By analyzing an individual's genetic makeup, doctors can tailor treatments to match the patient's specific genetic profile, maximizing the effectiveness of medications and minimizing potential side effects. This approach, known as pharmacogenomics, has the potential to revolutionize healthcare by providing personalized treatment plans based on an individual's unique genetic characteristics.

But what happens when genetic testing reveals the presence of a genetic disorder or a predisposition to a disease? This is where genetic counseling comes into play. Genetic counselors are professionals trained in both genetics and counseling, and they play a crucial role in helping individuals and families understand their test results, evaluate their risk, and make informed decisions about their health. Genetic counselors provide emotional support, help individuals navigate complex medical information, and guide them towards resources and support groups.

As students interested in genetics and genomics, it is essential to stay updated on the ethical and social implications of genetic testing. Issues such as privacy, confidentiality, and the potential misuse of genetic information need to be carefully considered. Understanding these aspects will help you navigate the field responsibly and advocate for ethical practices in genomic medicine.

In conclusion, genetic testing and counseling are essential components of the future of healthcare. As students interested in genetics and genomics, you are at the forefront of this exciting field. By exploring the potential of genetic testing and counseling, you can contribute to the development of personalized medicine and ensure the responsible and ethical use of genomic information.

# Rare Genetic Diseases

Genetics and Genomics play a vital role in understanding and unraveling the mysteries of human health and disease. In this subchapter, we will delve into the fascinating world of rare genetic diseases, exploring their causes, impact, and the groundbreaking research being conducted to combat them.

Rare genetic diseases, also known as orphan diseases, are a group of disorders that affect a small percentage of the population. While individually these diseases may be rare, collectively they impact millions of people worldwide. These conditions are often caused by mutations in specific genes, resulting in abnormal or missing proteins that disrupt the normal functioning of the body.

One example of a rare genetic disease is cystic fibrosis (CF), a life-threatening condition that primarily affects the lungs and digestive system. CF is caused by mutations in the CFTR gene, leading to the production of a faulty protein responsible for the build-up of thick, sticky mucus in various organs. Through advancements in genomics, researchers have made significant progress in understanding CF and developing innovative treatments aimed at improving the quality of life for those affected.

Another rare genetic disease is Hutchinson-Gilford progeria syndrome (HGPS), a condition that causes rapid aging in children. HGPS is caused by a mutation in the LMNA gene, resulting in the production of an abnormal protein called progerin. This protein causes cells to age prematurely, leading to a range of symptoms such as growth retardation, cardiovascular problems, and accelerated aging. Despite the challenges posed by HGPS, recent research has provided hope for potential treatments, with ongoing clinical trials exploring novel therapeutic approaches.

Rare genetic diseases pose unique challenges for patients, families, and healthcare providers. Due to their rarity, diagnosis can often be delayed or misdiagnosed, causing further distress to individuals and their loved ones. However, advancements in genetic testing technologies, such as whole-exome sequencing and gene panel testing, have revolutionized the diagnostic process, enabling more accurate and timely identification of these conditions.

Moreover, the field of genomics is constantly evolving, with researchers tirelessly working towards developing targeted therapies and personalized medicine for rare genetic diseases. Exciting breakthroughs, such as gene therapy, CRISPR-Cas9 gene editing, and RNA-based therapies, hold immense promise in treating and potentially curing these conditions.

As students interested in genetics and genomics, the study of rare genetic diseases offers a unique opportunity to contribute to the future of healthcare. By understanding the underlying genetic mechanisms and participating in research endeavors, you can play a vital role in improving the lives of individuals affected by these often-neglected conditions.

In conclusion, rare genetic diseases represent a significant challenge within the field of genomics. However, with ongoing advancements in technology and research, there is hope for improved diagnostic methods, novel treatments, and ultimately, better outcomes for patients. As students, you have the potential to be at the forefront of these discoveries, shaping the future of healthcare through your knowledge and dedication to the field of genetics and genomics.

## Infectious Disease Genomics

Infectious diseases have been a significant challenge to human health throughout history. However, with advancements in genomic medicine, we now have a powerful tool to understand, prevent, and treat these diseases more effectively. This subchapter, "Infectious Disease Genomics," explores the fascinating field of genomics in relation to infectious diseases, providing valuable insights for students interested in genetics and genomics.

Genomics, a branch of genetics, focuses on the study of an organism's complete set of DNA, including all of its genes. In the context of infectious diseases, genomics allows us to analyze the genetic material of pathogens like bacteria, viruses, and parasites. By understanding the genetic makeup of these infectious agents, we can gain crucial knowledge about their evolution, transmission, and drug resistance.

One of the most significant contributions of genomics to infectious disease research is the identification and tracking of outbreaks. Genomic sequencing enables scientists to identify and differentiate between strains of pathogens, helping trace the source and spread of infections. This information is vital in implementing timely public health interventions, such as quarantine measures and targeted vaccination campaigns.

Moreover, genomics also plays a crucial role in the development of vaccines and antiviral drugs. By studying the genetic makeup of pathogens, scientists can identify specific genes or proteins that are essential for their survival or virulence. This knowledge allows researchers to design vaccines that target these specific molecules, leading to more effective prevention strategies. Additionally, genomics helps in the discovery and development of antiviral drugs by identifying potential drug targets within the pathogen's genome.

Furthermore, genomics contributes to our understanding of antimicrobial resistance (AMR). AMR occurs when microorganisms evolve mechanisms to withstand the drugs used to treat infections, rendering them ineffective. Genomics research helps identify the genetic determinants responsible for drug resistance, allowing us to develop strategies to combat AMR more effectively. This knowledge is crucial in developing alternative treatment options and implementing rational use of antibiotics.

In conclusion, infectious disease genomics is an exciting and rapidly advancing field that offers tremendous potential for improving our ability to combat infectious diseases. By studying the genetic makeup of pathogens, genomics allows us to understand their evolution, track outbreaks, develop effective vaccines and drugs, and address the challenge of antimicrobial resistance. As students interested in genetics and genomics, exploring the world of infectious disease genomics will provide you with valuable insights into the future of healthcare and the critical role genomics plays in shaping it.

## Nutrigenomics and Lifestyle Factors

In this subchapter, we delve into the fascinating field of nutrigenomics and its relationship with lifestyle factors. As students in the realm of genetics and genomics, it is crucial to understand how our genes interact with the foods we consume and the lifestyle choices we make.

Nutrigenomics, also known as nutritional genomics, focuses on studying how individual genetic variations influence our response to nutrients and how our diet can impact gene expression. It explores the intricate connection between our genetic makeup and the foods we eat, shedding light on personalized nutrition and its potential implications for healthcare.

Lifestyle factors, such as physical activity, stress levels, sleep patterns, and environmental exposures, also play a significant role in shaping our gene expression. By understanding how these factors influence our genes, we can gain insights into how to optimize our health and well-being.

One of the key aspects of nutrigenomics is the concept of gene-diet interactions. Certain genetic variations can make individuals more susceptible to certain diseases or conditions, and diet plays a crucial role in either triggering or mitigating these risks. For instance, individuals with a certain gene variant may be more prone to developing heart disease, but a diet rich in fruits, vegetables, and whole grains can help reduce this risk.

Moreover, lifestyle factors can modify gene expression through a process called epigenetics. Epigenetic modifications, which do not alter the underlying DNA sequence, can be influenced by our environment and lifestyle choices. This means that even if we have certain genetic predispositions, we have the power to positively impact our health outcomes through lifestyle modifications.

Understanding the intricate relationship between nutrigenomics and lifestyle factors can empower us as students to make informed choices about our own health and enable us to become advocates for personalized healthcare. By incorporating this knowledge into patient care, healthcare professionals can provide tailored dietary and lifestyle recommendations to optimize health outcomes for individuals.

In conclusion, nutrigenomics and lifestyle factors are two interlinked areas that offer tremendous potential for revolutionizing healthcare. As students in genetics and genomics, we have a unique opportunity to explore and contribute to this field. By understanding how our genes interact with the foods we eat and the lifestyle choices we make, we can pave the way towards a future where personalized nutrition and lifestyle interventions are at the forefront of healthcare.

# Chapter 5: Genomic Medicine in Practice

## Clinical Implementation of Genomic Medicine

In recent years, the field of genomic medicine has made remarkable strides, revolutionizing the way we approach healthcare. The clinical implementation of genomic medicine has opened up new avenues for diagnosis, treatment, and prevention of various diseases, bringing hope to countless patients worldwide. In this subchapter, we will delve into the exciting realm of clinical implementation and explore how genomic medicine is transforming healthcare for the better.

Genomic medicine involves the use of an individual's genetic information to guide medical decisions. By analyzing an individual's DNA, scientists and healthcare professionals can gain valuable insights into their predisposition to certain diseases, their response to medications, and even potential risks for adverse reactions. This personalized approach allows for targeted and tailored interventions, leading to more effective and efficient healthcare outcomes.

One of the key areas where genomic medicine has made significant progress is in the diagnosis of genetic disorders. Through advanced sequencing technologies, clinicians can now identify specific gene mutations responsible for various genetic conditions. This not only aids in accurate diagnosis but also enables early intervention and management strategies. Moreover, genomic medicine has uncovered previously unknown disease-causing genes, expanding our understanding of rare genetic disorders and providing hope for affected individuals and their families.

Furthermore, genomic medicine has revolutionized the field of oncology. By analyzing the genetic makeup of a tumor, oncologists can identify specific mutations that drive the growth of cancer cells. This knowledge allows for the development of targeted therapies that directly inhibit these mutations, leading to more effective and personalized cancer treatments. Moreover, genomic medicine has paved the way for precision medicine in oncology, where treatment plans are tailored to an individual's unique genetic profile, improving outcomes and reducing side effects.

Beyond diagnosis and treatment, genomic medicine also plays a crucial role in preventive medicine. By identifying genetic risk factors, individuals can make informed lifestyle choices and undergo regular screenings to detect diseases at an early stage. Additionally, pharmacogenomics, a branch of genomic medicine, helps determine an individual's response to certain medications, minimizing adverse reactions and optimizing drug efficacy.

As students interested in genetics and genomics, it is crucial to stay abreast of the latest advancements in clinical implementation. Understanding the potential of genomic medicine and its impact on healthcare will not only broaden your knowledge but also equip you with the tools to contribute to this rapidly evolving field. By embracing genomic medicine, we can usher in a future where healthcare is truly personalized, precise, and patient-centric.

# Genomic Data Analysis and Interpretation

In the rapidly evolving field of genomics, the analysis and interpretation of genomic data play a crucial role in revolutionizing healthcare. As students venturing into the realms of genetics and genomics, understanding how to effectively analyze and interpret genomic data is of paramount importance. This subchapter will guide you through the process, equipping you with the necessary skills to navigate this exciting field.

Genomic data refers to the vast amount of information obtained from studying an individual's complete set of genes, known as the genome. This data holds immense potential in uncovering valuable insights into human health and disease. However, the sheer volume and complexity of genomic data pose significant challenges that need to be addressed through appropriate analysis and interpretation techniques.

To begin with, genomic data analysis involves several steps. It starts with data preprocessing, where raw sequencing data is cleaned, aligned, and organized. Next, various algorithms and statistical methods are employed to identify genetic variations, such as single nucleotide polymorphisms (SNPs) or structural variants. These variants are then annotated, meaning they are compared to existing databases to determine their potential impact on health and disease.

Once the genomic data is analyzed, the next step is interpretation. This involves connecting the genetic variations with relevant biological knowledge to understand their functional consequences. It is here that your understanding of genomics and genetics will be put to the test. By leveraging your knowledge of biological pathways, gene function, and disease mechanisms, you will be able to decipher the implications of these genetic variations.

In the field of genomics, interpretation also relies heavily on the integration of genomic data with clinical information, such as medical records and phenotypic data. This multidimensional approach allows for a more comprehensive understanding of the genetic basis of diseases and enables personalized medicine tailored to individual patients.

In this subchapter, you will explore various tools and resources used for genomic data analysis and interpretation. You will learn about bioinformatics, a discipline that combines biology and computer science to analyze and interpret genomic data. Additionally, you will gain insights into how genomic data analysis is transforming healthcare, from disease diagnosis to treatment selection.

By mastering the art of genomic data analysis and interpretation, you will be at the forefront of the genomic medicine revolution. You will contribute to the advancement of personalized healthcare, where treatments are tailored to an individual's unique genetic makeup. So, get ready to delve into the fascinating world of genomic data analysis and interpretation, and unlock the secrets hidden within our genes.

# Integrating Genomic Medicine into Healthcare Systems

In recent years, the field of genomics has revolutionized the way we understand and approach healthcare. Genomic medicine, the application of genomic information to guide medical decisions, holds tremendous promise for improving patient outcomes. As students interested in genetics and genomics, it is crucial to comprehend how the integration of this cutting-edge technology can transform healthcare systems.

One of the primary benefits of integrating genomic medicine into healthcare systems is the ability to personalize patient care. Traditionally, healthcare has followed a one-size-fits-all approach, but genomics allows for tailoring treatments to individual patients based on their unique genetic makeup. By analyzing an individual's genetic variations, healthcare professionals can predict disease susceptibility, identify optimal drug therapies, and develop personalized prevention strategies. This approach ensures that patients receive the most effective and targeted treatments, leading to better outcomes and reduced healthcare costs.

Furthermore, the integration of genomic medicine has the potential to revolutionize disease prevention. By identifying genetic predispositions, healthcare providers can implement proactive measures to prevent the onset of diseases before symptoms manifest. This proactive approach shifts the focus from treatment to prevention, ultimately reducing the burden on healthcare systems and improving population health.

Another crucial aspect of integrating genomic medicine is the impact it can have on drug development and precision medicine. Genomic data can uncover new drug targets, leading to the development of innovative therapies. Additionally, understanding a patient's genomic profile allows healthcare providers to prescribe medications that are tailored to their specific genetic makeup, maximizing efficacy and minimizing adverse reactions. This approach, known as precision medicine, represents a significant advancement in healthcare, moving away from a trial-and-error approach towards a more targeted and efficient treatment paradigm.

However, integrating genomic medicine into healthcare systems also presents challenges. The field is rapidly evolving, and healthcare professionals must continuously update their knowledge and skills to effectively incorporate genomics into practice. Additionally, issues related to data privacy and ethics arise when handling sensitive genetic information, necessitating robust policies and regulations to protect patient rights and ensure responsible use of genomic data.

In conclusion, integrating genomic medicine into healthcare systems offers immense potential for improving patient care, disease prevention, and drug development. As students interested in genetics and genomics, it is crucial to understand the transformative impact genomics can have on healthcare. By staying informed and actively participating in this evolving field, we can contribute to shaping the future of healthcare and promoting better outcomes for patients worldwide.

## Challenges and Future Directions of Genomic Medicine

As the field of genomic medicine continues to advance, it brings with it a myriad of challenges and promises for the future. This subchapter will explore some of the key challenges faced by researchers and healthcare professionals in this field, while also discussing the potential future directions of genomic medicine.

One of the primary challenges in genomic medicine is the interpretation of vast amounts of genetic data. With the advent of high-throughput sequencing technologies, it has become possible to rapidly sequence an individual's entire genome. However, the interpretation of this massive amount of data is not a simple task. Researchers and healthcare professionals must navigate through the complexities of genetic variations and their possible implications for an individual's health. This requires sophisticated computational tools and algorithms to analyze and interpret the data accurately.

Another challenge lies in ensuring privacy and security of genomic information. Genomic data is highly personal and sensitive, containing not only information about an individual's health but also their ancestry and potential risks for certain diseases. Safeguarding this information from unauthorized access and misuse is of utmost importance. Researchers and policymakers must work together to establish robust privacy regulations and maintain secure databases.

Additionally, the integration of genomic medicine into clinical practice is a significant challenge. While genomic testing and personalized medicine hold great promise, there is a need to educate healthcare professionals about the interpretation and application of genetic information. Medical school curricula should be updated to include genomics, ensuring that future doctors are equipped with the necessary knowledge and skills to incorporate genomic data into their practice.

Looking towards the future, genomic medicine holds immense potential for advancements in disease prevention, diagnosis, and treatment. The identification of disease-causing genetic mutations can lead to the development of targeted therapies, reducing the need for trial-and-error treatments. Furthermore, genomic medicine can enable predictive and preventive measures, allowing individuals to make lifestyle modifications and receive personalized interventions based on their genetic risks.

In the coming years, we can expect to see advancements in the field of pharmacogenomics, where medications are tailored to an individual's genetic profile, minimizing adverse side effects and increasing treatment efficacy. Genomic medicine may also revolutionize cancer treatment by identifying specific genetic mutations driving tumor growth and developing targeted therapies to combat them.

In conclusion, while genomic medicine presents numerous challenges, it also opens up exciting avenues for the future of healthcare. By addressing the challenges of data interpretation, privacy, and integration into clinical practice, researchers and healthcare professionals can harness the power of genomics to transform medicine. The future of genomic medicine holds great promise for personalized healthcare, disease prevention, and improved treatment outcomes, ultimately benefiting patients and society as a whole.

# Chapter 6: Ethics and Social Implications

**Privacy and Data Protection**

In today's digital age, where technology is rapidly advancing, the need for privacy and data protection has become more crucial than ever before. This subchapter aims to shed light on the significance of safeguarding personal information, especially in the context of genetics and genomics, for students interested in the future of healthcare.

As students exploring the field of genetics and genomics, you are likely to encounter vast amounts of sensitive data. This data may include personal health records, genetic test results, and other confidential information. It is essential to understand the importance of privacy and data protection to maintain the trust and ethical standards in this field.

Privacy is a fundamental human right that ensures individuals have control over their personal information. In healthcare, this becomes even more crucial as genetic information can reveal sensitive details about an individual's health, predispositions to diseases, and even their family history. Protecting this information is vital to prevent potential misuse or discrimination.

Data protection, on the other hand, focuses on safeguarding sensitive data from unauthorized access, use, or disclosure. In the realm of genetics and genomics, this involves implementing robust security measures to protect databases, genetic sequencing machines, and other technological infrastructure. Encryption, authentication, and access controls are some of the techniques employed to ensure data protection.

Regulatory frameworks, such as the General Data Protection Regulation (GDPR) in Europe and the Health Insurance Portability and Accountability Act (HIPAA) in the United States, have been established to govern the collection, storage, and sharing of personal data. Familiarizing yourself with these regulations is essential to ensure compliance and protect the privacy of individuals.

Additionally, the emergence of technologies like cloud computing and big data analytics brings both opportunities and challenges. While these technologies enable rapid data sharing and analysis, they also pose risks to privacy and data protection. It is imperative to be aware of the potential risks and take necessary precautions to minimize them.

In conclusion, privacy and data protection are of utmost importance in the field of genetics and genomics. As students, it is crucial to understand the ethical and legal implications surrounding the collection and use of personal information. By respecting privacy rights, adhering to regulatory frameworks, and implementing robust security measures, we can ensure the responsible and ethical use of genomic data in the future of healthcare.

## Genetic Discrimination

In our ever-evolving world, where advancements in healthcare and technology are revolutionizing the way we live, genetics and genomics have emerged as crucial fields that hold immense potential for the future of healthcare. These disciplines focus on the study of genes and their functions, aiming to decode the genetic makeup of individuals and understand how it contributes to their health and well-being. However, as we delve deeper into the realm of genetics, we must also address the ethical dilemmas that arise, one of the most significant being genetic discrimination.

Genetic discrimination refers to the unfair treatment of individuals based on their genetic information. This discrimination can occur in various areas, including employment, insurance, education, and even personal relationships. As students exploring the world of genetics and genomics, it is essential to understand the implications of genetic discrimination and work towards creating an inclusive and equitable society.

One area where genetic discrimination is particularly prevalent is in the workplace. Employers may make decisions about hiring, promotion, or termination based on an individual's genetic predisposition to certain diseases or conditions. This can lead to the exclusion of talented individuals from opportunities solely based on their genetic profile. As students, we must advocate for policies that protect individuals from such discrimination and promote equal opportunities for all.

Another area where genetic discrimination can occur is in the realm of health insurance. Insurance companies may deny coverage or charge higher premiums based on an individual's genetic information. This can result in individuals being unable to access the healthcare they need or facing financial burdens due to their genetic predispositions. As future healthcare professionals, it is crucial to advocate for policies that prohibit such discriminatory practices and ensure that everyone has equal access to affordable and quality healthcare.

Moreover, genetic discrimination can also impact an individual's personal relationships and social interactions. People may face stigmatization or exclusion from their communities due to their genetic makeup. As students, we have the power to educate others and promote acceptance and understanding of genetic differences. By fostering a culture of inclusivity, we can ensure that everyone is treated with dignity and respect, regardless of their genetic information.

In conclusion, genetic discrimination is a significant ethical concern in the field of genetics and genomics. As students exploring the future of healthcare, it is our responsibility to understand the implications of genetic discrimination and work towards creating a society that values and respects genetic diversity. By advocating for policies that protect individuals from discrimination, promoting equal opportunities, and fostering a culture of inclusivity, we can pave the way for a future where genetic discrimination is eradicated, and genomic medicine benefits all.

# Genetic Engineering and Designer Babies

In recent years, the field of genetics and genomics has witnessed incredible advancements, revolutionizing the way we understand and approach healthcare. One of the most intriguing and controversial aspects of this progress is genetic engineering and the concept of designer babies. This subchapter delves into the fascinating realm of genetic manipulation and its potential implications for the future of healthcare.

Genetic engineering refers to the deliberate alteration of an organism's genetic material, often done by introducing specific genes or modifying existing ones. This technique has opened up the possibility of creating "designer babies," individuals whose genes have been intentionally modified to enhance certain traits or eliminate genetic disorders.

At first glance, the idea of designing babies may seem like a concept straight out of science fiction. However, it is crucial for students in the field of genetics and genomics to understand the ethical, social, and scientific dimensions surrounding this topic. Genetic engineering and designer babies raise several complex questions that need careful consideration.

From an ethical standpoint, should parents have the right to decide their child's genetic makeup? What are the potential consequences of creating a society where genetic enhancement is the norm? These are just a couple of the profound ethical dilemmas that accompany the concept of designer babies, and exploring them allows students to develop a well-rounded understanding of the field.

Scientifically, genetic engineering holds immense potential for preventing hereditary diseases and improving human health. By eliminating harmful genetic mutations, it is possible to eradicate certain disorders from future generations. However, this also raises concerns about unintended consequences and the potential for unforeseen genetic complications.

Furthermore, social implications are intertwined with the advancement of genetic engineering. Will access to genetic enhancement be limited to the wealthy, exacerbating existing inequalities? How will this technology impact concepts of beauty, intelligence, and diversity in society? These questions push students to think critically about the broader implications of genetic engineering beyond the laboratory.

As students interested in genetics and genomics, it is essential to be well-informed about the possibilities and challenges presented by genetic engineering and designer babies. By dissecting the ethical, scientific, and social aspects, students can engage in informed discussions and shape the future of healthcare responsibly.

In conclusion, genetic engineering and designer babies represent a captivating yet controversial domain within the field of genomics. As students, it is imperative to explore this topic with an open mind, considering the ethical, scientific, and social dimensions. By doing so, we can contribute to the development of responsible and ethical applications of genetic engineering that benefit humanity as a whole.

## Access to Genomic Medicine

In recent years, the field of genomic medicine has made significant advancements, revolutionizing the way we diagnose, treat, and prevent diseases. Genomic medicine encompasses the use of a person's genetic information to guide medical decisions and interventions. As students interested in genetics and genomics, it is important for you to understand the concept of access to genomic medicine and its implications for the future of healthcare.

Access to genomic medicine refers to the ability of individuals to benefit from the latest genomic technologies and discoveries. It entails ensuring that all individuals, regardless of their socioeconomic background, have equal opportunities to utilize genomic information for personalized healthcare. However, access to genomic medicine is not yet universally available or affordable for everyone.

One of the major challenges in achieving widespread access to genomic medicine is the high cost associated with genetic testing and sequencing. While the costs have significantly reduced over the years, they are still prohibitive for many individuals and healthcare systems. Efforts are being made to develop more cost-effective technologies and strategies to make genomic testing accessible to all.

Another aspect of access to genomic medicine is the need for education and awareness. Students like you play a crucial role in bridging this gap. By educating yourselves about the potential of genomics in healthcare, you can help create awareness among your peers, families, and communities. This awareness can lead to increased demand for genomic testing and interventions, ultimately driving down costs and making it more accessible to everyone.

Furthermore, access to genomic medicine also depends on the availability of genomic data and information. Research studies and databases hold a wealth of genomic information that can be utilized for medical purposes. However, there are ethical and privacy concerns related to the sharing and utilization of this data. It is essential for researchers, policymakers, and healthcare professionals to work together to develop guidelines and policies that ensure the responsible use of genomic data while also prioritizing patient privacy and security.

In conclusion, access to genomic medicine is a crucial aspect of the future of healthcare. As students interested in genetics and genomics, it is important for you to be aware of the challenges and opportunities in this field. By advocating for equal access, educating others, and contributing to responsible genomic research, you can help shape a future where everyone can benefit from the power of genomic medicine.

# Chapter 7: The Future of Genomic Medicine

**Emerging Technologies and Innovations**

In the fast-paced world of healthcare, new technologies and innovations are constantly transforming the landscape of medicine. This subchapter on "Emerging Technologies and Innovations" aims to provide students with an insight into the exciting developments happening in the field of genetics and genomics.

One of the most significant advancements in recent years is the advent of genomic medicine. This revolutionary approach utilizes a person's unique genetic makeup to understand, diagnose, and treat diseases. With the help of advanced sequencing techniques, scientists can now decode an individual's entire genome, providing valuable insights into their health and predisposition to certain conditions.

Furthermore, the emergence of gene editing technologies, such as CRISPR-Cas9, has opened up new possibilities for genetic manipulation. Students will learn about how these tools can be used to modify genes, potentially correcting genetic abnormalities and preventing the development of inherited diseases.

Another area of innovation within genetics and genomics is personalized medicine. By analyzing a patient's genetic information, doctors can tailor treatment plans to suit their specific needs. This approach ensures that medications and therapies are more effective, minimizing adverse effects and improving patient outcomes.

Advancements in bioinformatics and data analysis have also played a crucial role in the field. Students will explore how big data and artificial intelligence are being utilized to mine vast amounts of genomic information and identify patterns and associations with diseases. This valuable knowledge can aid in the development of targeted therapies and precision medicine approaches.

Additionally, the rise of direct-to-consumer genetic testing companies has made genetic information more accessible to the general public. Students will gain an understanding of the benefits and ethical considerations surrounding these tests, as well as the importance of genetic counseling and interpretation of results.

As students delve into the chapter on "Emerging Technologies and Innovations," they will be encouraged to think critically about the potential implications and challenges associated with these advancements. Moreover, they will be inspired to explore career opportunities within the field of genetics and genomics, which are at the forefront of groundbreaking discoveries and life-changing interventions.

By staying informed about the latest developments in emerging technologies and innovations, students will be well-prepared to contribute to the future of healthcare and make a positive impact on the lives of patients worldwide.

# Genomic Medicine for Global Health

In the rapidly advancing field of healthcare, one area that holds immense promise for revolutionizing the way we understand and treat diseases is genomics. Genomic medicine, also known as personalized medicine, is a branch of medicine that focuses on using an individual's genetic information to tailor treatments and preventive measures. This subchapter will delve into the potential of genomic medicine in improving global health and its significance for students interested in genetics and genomics.

The impact of genomic medicine on global health cannot be overstated. By studying the genetic makeup of diverse populations worldwide, scientists can identify genetic variations that contribute to diseases and better understand their underlying mechanisms. This knowledge not only enables the development of more effective treatments but also facilitates the discovery of preventive strategies. Genomic medicine has the potential to transform the way diseases such as cancer, cardiovascular disorders, and rare genetic conditions are diagnosed and treated.

For students interested in genetics and genomics, understanding the principles and applications of genomic medicine is crucial. As future healthcare professionals and researchers, students will play a vital role in translating genomic discoveries into clinical practice. This subchapter will provide an overview of the fundamental concepts of genomics, including DNA sequencing, gene expression, and genetic variation analysis. It will also explore the ethical considerations and challenges associated with implementing genomic medicine on a global scale.

Furthermore, this subchapter will highlight the importance of collaboration and interdisciplinary approaches in genomic medicine. Genomics is a rapidly evolving field that requires expertise from various disciplines, such as genetics, bioinformatics, and computational biology. Students interested in genomics will have the opportunity to contribute to cutting-edge research and technological advancements that have the potential to improve global health outcomes.

In conclusion, genomic medicine holds immense potential for transforming healthcare and improving global health outcomes. This subchapter aims to equip students interested in genetics and genomics with the knowledge and understanding necessary to navigate this exciting field. By exploring the principles, applications, and challenges of genomic medicine, students will be prepared to contribute to the future of healthcare and make a positive impact on global health.

## Education and Training in Genomic Medicine

In a world where advancements in technology are reshaping the healthcare landscape, the field of genetics and genomics is at the forefront, revolutionizing how we diagnose and treat diseases. As students, it is crucial to understand the importance of education and training in genomic medicine to prepare ourselves for the future of healthcare.

Education in genomic medicine begins with a strong foundation in the sciences, particularly genetics and molecular biology. These subjects provide the fundamental knowledge needed to understand the complexities of genomics. Students interested in this field should focus on courses that delve into topics like DNA sequencing, gene expression, and genetic variation.

To gain a comprehensive understanding of genomic medicine, students can pursue specialized programs or degrees in genetics, genomics, or bioinformatics. These programs offer in-depth coursework and hands-on training in various aspects of genomic medicine. Additionally, they provide opportunities for students to engage in research projects, which can further enhance their knowledge and skills.

Training in genomic medicine goes beyond the classroom. Students can take advantage of internships or clinical rotations at research institutions or hospitals that specialize in genomics. These experiences allow students to work alongside experts in the field, gaining practical skills in genomic data analysis, genetic counseling, and the interpretation of genomic test results. Furthermore, students can participate in conferences and workshops that focus on the latest advancements in genomic medicine, providing them with valuable networking opportunities and exposure to cutting-edge research.

As the field of genomic medicine continues to evolve rapidly, staying up-to-date with the latest research and developments is crucial. Students should actively engage in continuing education through online courses, webinars, and scientific journals. This will ensure that they remain knowledgeable about emerging technologies, ethical considerations, and the impact of genomics on personalized medicine.

Ultimately, education and training in genomic medicine provide the foundation for students to become future leaders in the field. By acquiring a strong understanding of genetics and genomics, pursuing specialized programs, and engaging in practical experiences, students can develop the necessary skills and expertise to contribute to the advancements in genomic medicine.

In conclusion, the field of genomic medicine holds immense potential to revolutionize healthcare. As students interested in genetics and genomics, it is essential to prioritize education and training in this field. By doing so, we can become catalysts for change, shaping the future of healthcare and improving the lives of countless individuals through the power of genomics.

## Public Engagement and Genomic Literacy

In an era of rapid advancements in genetic and genomic medicine, it is more important than ever for students interested in genetics and genomics to understand the significance of public engagement and genomic literacy. The field of genetics and genomics holds immense potential in revolutionizing healthcare, but its successful implementation relies heavily on the active participation and understanding of the public.

Public engagement refers to involving the general public in discussions, decision-making processes, and actions related to genetic and genomic medicine. It is crucial to bridge the gap between scientists, healthcare professionals, and the public to ensure that the benefits of genomic medicine are maximized, while potential ethical, social, and legal implications are addressed.

One of the key aspects of public engagement is genomic literacy, which refers to the understanding of basic genetic and genomic concepts by individuals. Genomic literacy empowers individuals to make informed decisions about their health, participate in research, and contribute to public discourse on genetic and genomic issues. As students interested in genetics and genomics, developing genomic literacy is essential not only for your own understanding but also for effectively communicating complex concepts to the public.

Understanding the ethical, legal, and social implications of genetic and genomic medicine is another vital component of public engagement. As future researchers, healthcare providers, or policymakers, students must be aware of the potential challenges and controversies surrounding the field. By actively engaging in discussions and debates, students can contribute to shaping policies that strike a balance between scientific advancements and societal concerns.

Public engagement can take various forms, from participating in community outreach programs and science fairs to using social media platforms to disseminate accurate information about genetic and genomic medicine. It is through these efforts that students can promote genomic literacy and encourage public involvement in the decision-making processes.

By actively engaging with the public, students interested in genetics and genomics can pave the way for a future where the benefits of genomic medicine are accessible to all. As you embark on your journey in this exciting field, remember that your knowledge and efforts can make a significant impact on shaping the future of healthcare.

# Chapter 8: Conclusion and Reflections

## Summary of Key Concepts

In this subchapter, we will provide a summary of the key concepts covered in "The Future of Healthcare: Exploring Genomic Medicine for Students." This book is specifically designed for students with an interest in the fields of genetics and genomics, aiming to introduce them to the exciting world of genomic medicine and its potential impact on healthcare.

1. Introduction to Genomic Medicine: We begin by explaining the fundamental concepts of genomic medicine, exploring how the study of genes and genomes can revolutionize healthcare. Students will learn about the Human Genome Project and how it has paved the way for personalized medicine.

2. Understanding Genes and Genomes: This section dives deeper into the structure and function of genes and genomes. Students will gain an understanding of DNA, RNA, and the role of genes in determining an individual's traits and susceptibility to diseases.

3. Genetic Variation and Inheritance: Here, we explore the concept of genetic variation and how it affects inheritance patterns. Students will learn about Mendelian genetics, genetic disorders, and the role of genetic counseling in identifying and managing inherited conditions.

4. Genomic Technologies: This section introduces students to the cutting-edge technologies used in genomics research and healthcare. Topics include DNA sequencing, gene editing tools like CRISPR-Cas9,

and bioinformatics techniques used to analyze large-scale genomic data.

5. Genomic Medicine Applications: We highlight the various applications of genomic medicine in healthcare. Students will discover how genomics is shaping the diagnosis, treatment, and prevention of diseases such as cancer, cardiovascular disorders, and rare genetic conditions.

6. Ethical, Legal, and Social Implications: Genomic medicine raises important ethical, legal, and social questions. We discuss issues such as privacy, genetic discrimination, and the impact of genomic research on diverse populations. Students will be encouraged to think critically about these complex topics.

7. Future Directions: The final section explores the future of genomic medicine, discussing emerging technologies, ongoing research, and potential advancements in healthcare. Students will gain insight into the possibilities and challenges that lie ahead in this rapidly evolving field.

"The Future of Healthcare: Exploring Genomic Medicine for Students" aims to inspire young minds to pursue careers in genetics and genomics while equipping them with the foundational knowledge needed to understand and contribute to the exciting field of genomic medicine.

## Personal Reflections on Genomic Medicine

As students exploring the fascinating world of genetics and genomics, we are privileged to witness the rapid advancements and groundbreaking discoveries in the field of genomic medicine. The potential it holds for revolutionizing healthcare is truly awe-inspiring. In this subchapter, we delve into personal reflections on genomic medicine – our thoughts, experiences, and the impact it has on our lives.

Genomic medicine has unlocked the door to a deeper understanding of our genetic makeup, offering insights into our predispositions for certain diseases, personalized treatment plans, and even the potential for preventive measures. For many of us, this knowledge has sparked a sense of wonder and curiosity about our own genetic heritage. We find ourselves contemplating questions like: What makes us who we are? How do our genes influence our health? How can we harness this knowledge to improve patient outcomes?

One of the most striking aspects of genomic medicine is its potential to transform the way we approach healthcare. It empowers us to move away from the traditional one-size-fits-all model and towards a more personalized and tailored approach. By analyzing our genetic data, healthcare providers can identify specific genetic variations that may impact our response to medications or increase our susceptibility to certain diseases. This knowledge allows for targeted interventions and treatments, leading to better outcomes and improved quality of life.

Moreover, genomic medicine offers tremendous potential in the realm of preventive medicine. Armed with information about our genetic predispositions, we can make proactive lifestyle choices to mitigate our risks. This might involve adopting healthier habits, undergoing regular screenings, or even considering preventive surgeries in certain cases. By taking charge of our genetic health, we have the power to shape our future and make informed decisions that positively impact our well-being.

However, as we explore the possibilities of genomic medicine, ethical considerations come to the forefront. The access and privacy of our genetic information, the potential for discrimination based on genetic profiles, and the responsibility of healthcare providers to navigate these complexities are all crucial aspects that require careful thought and regulation. We must strike a balance between the immense potential of genomic medicine and the ethical boundaries that protect individuals' rights and privacy.

In conclusion, genomic medicine presents an exciting frontier in healthcare for students like us, passionate about genetics and genomics. It opens doors to new possibilities, challenges our understanding of human health, and forces us to reflect on the ethical implications it brings. As we continue our journey of exploration, let us embrace the potential of genomic medicine while remaining grounded in the principles of responsible and ethical practice, for the future of healthcare lies within our hands.

www.ingramcontent.com/pod-product-compliance
Lightning Source LLC
LaVergne TN
LVHW052002060526
838201LV00059B/3799